LIFE AGAIN

ERIC A. WILLIAMS

Published By:
Jasher Press & Co.
www.jasherpress.com
customerservice@jasherpress.com
1.888.220.2068
P.O. Box 14520
New Bern, NC 28561

Copyright© 2015
Interior Text Design by Pamela S. Almore
Cover Design by Pamela S. Almore

ISBN: 978-0692356326

First Edition
Printed and bound in the United States of America

TABLE OF CONTENTS

DEDICATION

"There is no influence so powerful
as that of the mother. . . "
-Sarah Josepha Hale

I dedicate this book to the memory of my
mother, Patricia Willoughby Williams. You
may have people to step in as your mother,
but you only get one. I truly thank God for my
mother who was a constant source of guidance,
encouragement and strength. She left my life too
soon.

ACKNOWLEDGEMENTS

I know that God will send people in our lives to help us to fulfill the purpose that He has created for us, not only sending people but allows us to be born to a particular family. God has graciously blessed me with an awesome, amazing and astonishing wife, Iris J. Williams. My children have added another level of blessings to my life; they are GREAT and GRAND - Erica, Alexis, Eric and Jalen. I cannot forget about my grandson BJ. Family members are not chosen, we are born into a family. God has allowed me to be born into one of the BEST families every. Thanks to Thaddeus and Marie Willoughby, my grandparents, for such great love, support and encouragement. And thanks to the rest of my family also.

When God places a person in your life and that person's very being is to help you get closer to God, that person should have a special place in your heart. God put Bishop Darryl S. Brister in my life to help me to become the Pastor, Leader, and Man I am today. To my BLIM family and my covenant brothers, thanks for all of your support and unconditional love. To Jaworski Sartin, thanks for all that you do.

I am so grateful to God that He permitted me to be born to such a compassion mother, Patricia Willoughby. She instilled so many valuable and unforgettable lessons of life in me, she will NEVER be forgotten. I dedicated this book to my beloved mother, Patricia Willoughby.

FOREWORD

"LIFE AGAIN" by Eric A. Williams
Bishop Darryl S. Brister

Our honesty with the Father doesn't reveal anything to HIM that HE doesn't already know! HIS intellect is so keen that HE doesn't have to wait for you to make a mistake. HE knows of your failure before you fail. HIS knowledge is all-inclusive, spanning the gaps between times and incidents. HE knows our thoughts even as we unconsciously gather them together to make sense in our own mind! I'm both humbled and honored to see the wonderful redemptive work that GOD has done in the life and ministry of my son in the faith, Pastor Eric A. Williams. This wonderful work and testimony "Life Again" will do just that; give men, women, boys and girls a desire to live again!

Success in your life depends on you. It depends on your relationship with God. Your attitudes toward life, your belief system and the thoughts, words, and actions you choose to govern your life daily! You are, quite simply, the person shaping your own destiny. Whatever path you choose in your life will be a free choice. You have made it for better or worse! This book gives unto all who read it a new lease on life. The courage it takes in sharing such personal experiences is simply encouraging. Sometimes Christians become frustrated and withdraw from activity on the basis of personal struggles. They think it's all over, but God says not so! The best is yet to come. The Lord doesn't like pity parties, and those who have them are shocked to find that although He is invited, He seldom attends.

In the crucible of His wisdom and the ecology of His grace, God has ordered some trouble for you today.

11

And every day of your life. We've been blessed with difficulties. Yes, you read right—blessed! The worst thing that could happen to us would be not to have any difficulties. If that were the case, we'd never know our need of the Lord. So God in essence says, "I'm going to give you sufficient difficulty for the day." God gives you enough difficulty to draw you close to Him, but then God gives you enough grace to meet those difficulties every day.

Is there a difficult circumstance in your life? If so, thank God for sending it your way to make you more like Jesus. Now ask for His grace to be victorious through it! The thing that gives a man power to rise above his circumstances is his coming to himself. You feel fulfilled when you achieve a sense of belonging through your job, family, or ministry.

Who you choose to do life with determines your future. If you choose to walk with the wise, then according to GOD's Word you will be wise; but the companion of fools will be destroyed or "will suffer harm" (as translated in the NIV). GOD has given Eric A. Williams wisdom beyond his years. According to biblical understanding, he is wise. A wise person is one who sees life for how it is and makes decisions based on how life really is rather than on how he or she hopes it would somehow be.

"Life Again" is more than thought-provoking. It is a must-read for any belief system, class, religion, or gender. Son, protege, and friend thanks again for stretching many of us yet again and challenging us to leave our comfort zones.

Bishop Darryl S. Brister

INTRODUCTION

Each moment in life leads to the next moment. Sometimes we deviate from our divine course, and choose to do things our way, leading us down a path of disappointments, heartaches, trials and tribulations. Even in the midst of our mistakes, there is still hope. God will use our misery and cause it to become our ministry. This has become my testimony. The things and life situations that once had me bound and broken have taught me valuable lessons, allowed me to encourage those who are experiencing similar trials, and warn others of the traps and pitfalls that lie ahead when we chose to live outside of God's will.

I'll set the scene for my testimony, Life Again, by sharing my childhood memories. My life began in 1968 when I was born to a teenage mother in New Orleans, Louisiana. When I was about two years old, my mom, Patricia Willoughby, met and married the man who I thought was my father. I would later learn that he was not my biological father. However, I thank God for him because he adopted me, gave me his last name, and raised me as my very own son. My earliest years were spent with my grandparents, Thaddeus and Marie Willoughby. I lived with them until I was about six years old. At that time, my grandmother thought that it would be best for me to live with my parents and two younger sisters, Monique and Christina.

I attended St. Paul the Apostle School, a private school, for eight years. My grandmother mentioned to my mom that I should attend a private school because it would provide the structure that I needed. I wasn't a bad kid, but some would say that I was mischievous. That's why I needed to be educated in a structured environment. While there I profited more than mere discipline; God was instilled in me.

There's an old saying that says some people are born leaders while others are taught to be leaders. I believe God allowed me to be born a leader. From first grade to fifth, I was a representative on the Student Council for my class. After completing eighth grade, I went to a public high school, Abramson Senior High School, where I continued to show great leadership by becoming the captain of the basketball team and a member of the Christian Athletes Program. Now in hind sight, I can see that the hand of God was on my life even as a kid. Sometimes I went to church even when my parents didn't go.

Eventually, our lives come full circle, and we return to the place where God always wanted us to be. It's a place where we reconnect with our beginnings. When we make that connection, we can define and fully live out our purpose. For me, that circle encompasses a deep love for God and the ability to lead people. This book sketches my

14

journey in life. In "Life Again," I'll discuss the things that took life away from me, but I will also tell of the things that gave me life once again.

CHAPTER 1

MY WILL VS. GOD'S WILL

Like most people, I was on a quest for the "American Dream." I wanted a family, a big house, a nice car, and a rewarding career. All of that was good, but God was not concerned about my achievements. He was concerned about who I was becoming. Becoming allows us to experience hard lessons in life. God never said that our journey would be easy, but He did promise to guide us through it all. The Bible records, "I have told you these things, so that in me you may have peace. In this world you will have trouble. But take heart! I have overcome the world (John 16:33)."

In order to achieve my goals, I developed a plan that began with getting a college education. I went to college in hopes of endless job opportunities. Upon graduating from high school, my mom sat me down at the table and asked me what I planned to study in college. "I want to major in Business," I replied. "I just love people. I love being around people." I never in a million years would have thought that my heart for people would lead me to where I am today.

With a plan and ambition, I enrolled in the nearby Delgado Community College and studied there for a year before transferring to Southern University at New Orleans where I majored in Business. While in college, I worked for a company called Popeye's for several years. In fact, I began working there while I was in high school.

I moved up in the company rather quickly, being promoted to a manager's position at the age of 21. I was one of the youngest managers that Popeye's had ever promoted. I eventually became a general manager and was making decent money. I enjoyed working with my fellow coworkers as well as the people who we served. I was blessed to meet some of the people who are still a part of my life today. I was also fortunate to work alongside Al Copeland, Jr., being a part of the SOS (Store Open Specialists) Team. Working in management at Popeye's was beneficial to my development as a leader.

I continued to excel as a leader within Popeye's and was given the opportunity to move to Atlanta, Georgia, to manage an existing restaurant. I moved my wife and daughter there, and we lived there for about two years. While living there, we were members of New Birth Missionary Baptist Church where Bishop Eddie Long was the pastor. We eventually moved back to Louisiana. Moving back home was part of God's developmental plan for me. It was His strategy to get me where He desired me to be. When I returned home, ministry really began for me.

God will sometimes interrupt our plans in order to build His kingdom and get us to our destiny. Think about the Virgin Mary. She was in the midst of planning her wedding when the angel Gabriel appeared to her saying that she would give birth to our Savior. Life is a never-ending series of choices. We can either chose to do things our way, or we can fulfill the will of God. What if Mary would have had an abortion? As God's chosen people, we must accept God's plan for our lives. It's His favor that has set us apart, even when we may seem less than great in the eyesight of others. Mary was a poor maid servant, yet she was chosen by God.

Upon our return, I became a member of Beacon Light International Cathedral under the leadership of Bishop Darryl Brister. I began serving in the church and was later ordained as a Deacon. Soon enough, I accepted my call to ministry in 1994, saying that God had called me to minister the Gospel to His people. In 1996, I was licensed to preach, and I was ordained as an Elder of the church the following year. It was at this point that I realized the seriousness of ministry and that I would be doing this for the rest of life, helping to manifest God's vision. My experiences would come to validate my place in ministry and the mission that God has assigned to my life.

My heart's desire was to continue to work in management. I was content with my aspirations to climb the corporate ladder, and I was making it happen. Situations that were out of my control brought me back home. At this point, it seemed as if my desires had been ruled out, making them nearly impossible to achieve. I always knew that God had a special purpose and plan for my life; however, I never included Him in my plans. I was like Jonah who heard the voice of God, but chose to disobey. Many of us are familiar with the character, plot and story of Jonah. His story involves the Lord, Jonah, other people (pagan), a ship, a fish, and a great storm. Jonah, like many of us, made a bad decision that caused his life to derail. The first four verses of scripture in the first book of Jonah records,

> DIFFICULTIES ARE DIVINELY DESIGNED TO DEVELOP AND TO BRING US INTO OUR DESTINY.

1 The word of the Lord came to Jonah son of Amittai:

² "Go to the great city of Ninevehand preach against it, because its wickedness has come up before me."

³ But Jonah ran away from the Lord and headed for Tarshish. He went down to Joppa, where he found a ship bound for that port. After paying the fare, he went aboard and sailed for Tarshish to flee from the Lord.

⁴ Then the Lord sent a great wind on the sea, and such a violent storm arose that the ship threatened to break up.

Jonah's disobedience caused a storm to arise in his life. Disobeying the Word of God and wisdom of God are two sure ways to cause storms in our lives. When we choose to do what we want to do, we will find ourselves going down, and we will pay to go down. It will always cost. We cannot run from God because of his omnipresent power; He is everywhere. When we find ourselves in storms of God, we must deal with them if we are going to get our lives back on track. It is important for us to realize that all storms are not an attack of Satan. Many are self-imposed, and some are sent by God and are a part of His permissible will.

God sent a storm to reprimand Jonah in love. The good news is that God's chastening is not designed to destroy us; discipline affirms His love for us. Difficulties are divinely designed to develop and to bring us into our destiny. This storm did not prove to be fatal for Jonah because he was given another chance after the storm.

CHAPTER 2

A LIFE SEEMINGLY GONE WRONG

"**B**aby, whatever you do, trust in the Lord, and lean not to your own understanding. But in all of your ways acknowledge Him, and He shall direct your path." As I laid face down on the bed in my grandmother's house with tears streaming from my eyes, my mother gently spoke those words into my life. I had reached one of the lowest points in my life. In that moment, I was lifeless and without hope. My life had gotten so far off track that I wasn't sure of how to put things back in order or where to even start. That's why I thank God for my mother who knew that better days were ahead for me, but I had to first trust God.

I think it would have been easy to blame my misfortune on others, but many of my problems had grown out of a series of bad choices that I had made. I was twenty-something years old, divorced, living with my grandmother, parenting two baby girls, Erica and Alexis, and unemployed. It had seemed as if my life had gone wrong. I watched every dream of mine fall apart before my very eyes. There was no big house and no fancy car. My family was scattered, and I didn't even have a job. My "American Dream" had become a "Nightmare on Elm Street."

In verse seven of the first chapter of Jonah, it says that they began to cast lots because they were trying to determine who caused the storm, and it fell upon Jonah. Jonah was the cause of the storm. In these moments of discipline, God is perfecting our lives. He is maturing us. During my difficulties, God was helping me get myself together and was preparing me for my next blessing.

God desires for us to have something on the inside of us that will keep us during our trials and tribulations. That something is His Word which we should embed in our hearts so that we may not sin against Him. It is not our design to let our gifts and talents take us where our character can't keep us. That's why we must be prepared before God promotes us.

The dissolution of my marriage was, in hind sight, an awakening moment for me. At the end of my marriage, I was able to acknowledge that I wasn't ready for marriage. I was about 22 years old when I got married. I was still figuring out who I was, and I thought I knew who I wanted to be. There's a level of spiritual and mental maturity that is needed to maintain a marriage. I was lacking both.

Of course, I made attempts to repair the damage that I had caused to my marriage, but things were too far gone. I believe that there are no limits to what God can do, but at that time in my life my faith wasn't where it is today. A broken marriage is nothing for God to fix. However, we must be prepared to receive His favor and His grace. Imagine if God had healed my broken marriage before giving me the heart of a husband. My then wife and I would always return to a state of broken hearts.

After my wife divorced me, I moved into one of the spare bedrooms at my grandmother's house. This was a humbling experience for me. I was a grown man who was living with his grandmother. I can remember sitting in the living room watching an interior decorating program on TV with my grandmother. I leaned over and told her that the pillows that were being showcased on the television program were nice. I knew then that it was time for me to get my life together. I was a grown man, watching an interior decorating television program in the middle of the day with my grandmother, and complementing throw pillows. It's okay to laugh. It's funny to me now that I look back on it. It was just that bad. I had to get myself together.

> IT'S TRUE THAT THE DECISIONS THAT WE MAKE NOT ONLY AFFECT OUR LIVES BUT ALSO THE LIVES OF OTHERS WHO WE ARE CONNECT TO.

It's true that the decisions that we make not only affect our lives but also the lives of others who we are connect to. I was not married and was now the father of a second child. My daughter Alexis was born during a time when my life was in disarray. To top it all off, I was still trying to figure out fatherhood. It was very difficult to parent two baby girls in two separate households, neither of which I lived.

Life for me seemed so bleak at times that the enemy would tell me to take my own life. I would be driving home sometimes, and the devil would tell me to hit the fire hydrant. I knew that wasn't the answer. In due time, the things that weighed me down would break. I just wanted to know when that time would come. How long was this storm going to last?

> THE TRUTH OF THE MATTER IS WHEN WE DON'T HAVE FINANCIAL PROBLEMS WE DON'T HAVE MANY PROBLEMS AT ALL.

Because I was experiencing financial problems, my car was being repossessed. I had a nice ride too. It was Nissan Maxima. The sad part is that there were times when I would park my car down the street from my grandmother's house to hide it from the repo man. I have to admit that God showed me favor as it relates to my vehicle being repossessed. I was able to duck and dodge the collectors for nearly a year. Eventually, I returned the car one day after work and left the keys in the vehicle.

I think the fact that I had financial troubles magnified the other issues that I was dealing with. "A feast is made for laughter, And wine makes merry; But money answers everything

(Ecclesiastes 10:19)." The truth of the matter is when we don't have financial problems we don't have many problems at all. The lack of money had me depressed and on edge.

In the midst of all of my personal struggles, my mother went home to be with the Lord at the age of 51. Her death was unexpected and sudden. She died of heart failure. God allowed me to be there by her side when she made her transition, being able to return the amazing gift that He had

> ALWAYS REMEMBER THAT SUPERSTAR ATHLETES MUST SOMETIMES PLAY IN THE GAME HURT.

given me back into His care. Somehow I was able to cope with the loss of my mom. Somewhere I found strength to move forward. God strengthened me daily, and at her funeral service, I was able to deliver the eulogy.

No one can hang a sign outside their door that says "No Hurt Here". Many of us try our best to ignore our pain. Whether it is physical, emotional, psychological or spiritual, we try to cover or deaden the pain with alcohol, drugs, sex, food or even work. Instead, we should face the pain, get an understanding of the pain and fight through it. When others are depending on us we have to fight through the dysfunctions in our relationships, bad financial decisions, the loss of a loved one, or the loss of a job. Always remember that superstar athletes must sometimes play in the game hurt. For example, there were times when Michael Jordan had to play games with a sprained ankle.

I had to fight through the pain because my daughters were depending on me. I had to cleave to the Word of God. Second Samuel 23:10 speaks of Eleazar who was a leader of David's mighty men and was famous for hanging with David in a famous battle against the Philistines. Even when his hand was weary, his hand stuck to the sword. Through his tenacity the LORD brought about a great victory (2 Samuel 23:10). Eleazar had a literal sword, but our sword is the Word of God. To defeat the enemy, I had to dig deep. I had to dig deep on the inside and recall His Word which says that no weapon formed against me shall prosper.

The caveat to this story is that all of this occurred after I became saved and while I was working in ministry! Although I was serving God and His people, there were some realities that I needed to grasp. Charles Spurgeon said it best when he said, "God does not allow His children to sin successfully." Instead he leads us to repentance.

CHAPTER 3

LOST IN THE REALITY OF MINISTRY

Ministry is a journey. It's a personal calling to serve God's people as He directs our paths from one place to another. Throughout the journey, God has his hands upon us as our source of strength and protection. At our very conception, God begins to prepare and cultivate us for our life's work. The scriptures record, "Before I formed you in the womb I knew you; Before you were born I sanctified you; I ordained you a prophet to the nations (Jeremiah 1:5)." My preparation began while I was attending a Catholic school. As a young boy, I began learning spiritual principles that have sustained me.

Christian ministry is meeting the needs of God's people. In the New Testament, ministry is seen as service to God and to other people in His name. Jesus drafted the blueprint for Christian

> I BELIEVE YOU CAN NEVER AMOUNT TO WHAT YOU HAVEN'T BEEN EXPOSED TO.

ministry. "For even the Son of Man did not come to be served, but to serve, and to give His life a ransom for many (Mark 10:45)."

Everyone's journey is not the same. However, we begin in the same manner. Each starts with salvation, accepting Christ as our Lord and Savior. At the age of 19, I accepted the Lord as my personal savior at Greater St. Stephens Full

Gospel Baptist Church under the leadership of Bishop Paul S. Morton. That's when my walk with Christ began.

It's funny how God has always exposed me to large ministries. I have never been a part of a small church. Even when I was in Atlanta, I was a part of a large ministry. I believe you can never amount to what you haven't been exposed to. I thank God for the exposure that my journey has afforded me.

After being in Atlanta for several years, God allowed me to move back home. Upon my return, I discovered that Bishop Darryl Brister was pastoring a church called Beacon Light in the city of New Orleans. I really didn't know him personally, but I knew of him from the days when I was a member of Greater St. Stephens. We were there at the same time. I decided to visit Beacon Light. After about two visits, I knew that was the place where God wanted me to be.

As a member of Beacon Light, I began to become engaged in the Word of God and the things of God. I began to see ministry in a new light. It began to take on a new form. It was servanthood. Eventually, I began serving as a deacon and was ordained. I worked as a deacon for a while before becoming a minister.

Being a deacon was my first encounter with leadership in the church. I had operated in leadership roles outside of ministry but never in the church. Whether it's secular leadership or leadership in ministry, leadership starts within the heart. Serving can be taught; however, if it is not heartfelt, it will end quickly. It is important to note that

> WE MUST ALWAYS DO WHAT WE DO FOR THE LORD.

leadership doesn't have a particular appearance. Many judge others on their physical appearance. According to 1 Samuel 16:7, God does not see as man sees. Man looks at the outward appearance, but the Lord looks at the heart. It all starts in the heart (Psalm 19:14). I enjoyed serving in the ministry and became a servant-leader. I use the term "servant-leader" because my natural feeling is to serve others first.

The quality of our leadership is a direct result of our spiritual preparation. As servant-leaders, we must first commit to God. We see this teaching in Matthew 22:37-40:

> Jesus said to him, "'You shall love the Lord your God with all your heart, with all your soul, and with all your mind.'
>
> [38] This is the first and great commandment.
>
> [39] And the second is like it: 'You shall love your neighbor as yourself.'
>
> [40] On these two commandments hang all the Law and the Prophets."

Whatever we commit ourselves to is what we become, i.e. a great husband, a great wife, an awesome coach, a good supervisor, an effective minister, a hospitable greeter, or a self-less deacon. Commitment goes pass love. We must always do what we do for the Lord. Colossians 3:22-24 tells us that we should be sincere in our actions with no hidden motives:

[22] Bondservants, obey in all things your masters according to the flesh, not with eyeservice, as men-pleasers, but in sincerity of heart, fearing God.

[23] And whatever you do, do it heartily, as to the Lord and not to men, [24] knowing that from the Lord you will receive the reward of the inheritance; for you serve the Lord Christ.

Many people do things for all the wrong reasons. Some are motivated by "eye service," serving only to be seen by others. Others are men pleasers and want to please everyone. As servant leaders, we must also lead by example. We must constantly work hard to be living examples of Christ. "But Jesus said to him, 'No one, having put his hand to the plow, and looking back, is fit for the kingdom of God (Luke 9:62).'" I'm not saying that we have to be perfect, but I am saying that we cannot expect others to do things that we will not do ourselves.

Even though I was fulfilling the work of the Lord, I still felt like there was more work for me to do. I felt that God had called me to preach the Word. Before becoming a minister, I would always travel with Bishop Brister, serving as his armorbearer. He would tell me that the way that I was with him was the same way that he was with Bishop Morton. That's when I knew that God was calling me to preach the Gospel.

I can remember telling Bishop Brister that I was called to minister. I called him on the phone and expressed the need to share something with him. When I arrived at his house, the man of God already had his Bible open. He asked me if what I was about to tell him had been shared with anyone else. I replied that I hadn't told anyone. I began to tell him that God had called me into ministry, and he said that he already knew it. He said that he was just waiting on me to answer the call.

The title of my first sermon was "Comfort Zones." The sermon was centered on Moses coming out of his comfort zone. Often times when I look back over my life, I see where God put me in certain situations where I had to get out of my comfort zone. In 1996, I was licensed as a minister by my pastor. After showing growth and maturity, I was ordained as an Elder just one year later. I thank God for the times that I was allowed to minster at Beacon Light of New Orleans. Those opportunities allowed me to grow. I was later appointed as the New Members' Pastor. I really enjoyed working with the new members, and it became my passion. We watched the church grow from hundreds to thousands. I felt blessed to be a part of a great church with an anointed leader.

While everything seemed to be going well on the forefront, I still had struggles that I was battling behind the scenes. Many would like to paint the picture that working in ministry is easy, but that's not totally true. Someone once said, "To serve God realistically, we must learn to wait on Him, to work with people, and to wrestle with problems." When there's love for God and a genuine love for His people, the easy part is serving. The difficult part is dealing with our own personal issues.

The enemy wanted my faith, because he knows that without faith it is impossible to please God. At one point it seemed as if these struggles began to overtake me while I was working in ministry. "My brethren, count it all joy when you fall into various trials (James 1:2)." Finding joy in the midst of my trial was no small feat. During those difficult moments, I was very emotional which made life's situations hard to deal

> I CAME TO LEARN THAT JUST AS THERE IS LIFE AFTER DEATH, THERE IS LIFE AFTER DIVORCE.

with. When James says "count it all joy," he is not talking about an emotional reaction but a deliberate appraisal of the situation from God's perspective. I was in a constant battle with the enemy. This was, perhaps, the toughest part of my journey.

As the New Members' Pastor, I went through a divorce. It was very difficult and embarrassing to go through publicly. There were times that I thought I wasn't going to survive. I came to learn that just as there is life after death, there is life after divorce. Even with my mistakes and bad choices, God still had a plan for my life. The decisions or choices that I made not only affected me, but also everyone who was connected to me. It lead to me losing my full-time job at Beacon Light of New Orleans.

When we fall (sin) or make mistakes, our trials are predictable. Knowing the calling that was upon my life and the course that I had chosen to take, I was bound to steer directly into a storm. The fact that trials are predictable lets us know that it's a part of the pilgrimage through life. There are at least two types of trials, trials of perfection and trials of correction. Trials of correction are a

> PATIENCE LOOKS FORWARD TO BETTER THINGS. IT LOOKS BEYOND TODAY'S CLOUDS AND AWAITS TOMORROW'S SUNSHINE.

result of being out of the will of God. An example of this is when Jonah disobeyed God and found himself in a storm (trial). On the other hand, trials of perfection come to fortify our faith and draw us closer to God. Perfection is not a sense of being faultless or without sin but rather a state of maturity.

In the midst of our troubles, God will correct and perfect our lives. I was praying like never before, asking God for forgiveness and guidance. I was like Jonah who cried out to the Lord in distress, "And he said: 'I cried out to the Lord because of my affliction, And He answered me. Out of the belly of Sheol I cried, *And* You heard my voice (Jonah 2:2).'"

Trials are also problematic, disrupting the normal flow of life. My problems had seemingly creating a falling domino effect. I was being faced with one problem after

> PERFECTION IS NOT A SENSE OF BEING FAULTLESS OR WITHOUT SIN BUT RATHER A STATE OF MATURITY.

another. I was divorced, my second child was to be born soon, I was unemployed, my car was being repossessed, and I was living with my grandmother. In other words, I was homeless because I didn't have a home of my own. I had lost my wife, my home, and my job, but none of that compared to the loss of my mother. I was devastated. Words really can't express the hurt that I felt. (I'll talk about how I coped with my mother going home to be with the Lord a little later.)

Although trials are predictable and problematic, trials are also paradoxical. Paradoxical means to seemingly be absurd or self-contradictory. In other words, paradoxical is something that just doesn't make sense. This is seen in verse 2 of James Chapter 1. When we are going through trials, we should have joy, knowing that there is purpose behind every trial.

In order to have joy, or gladness of heart, we must look past our troubles. James 1:3 says that our testing produces patience. Patience looks forward to better

> WE STILL HAVE TO DEAL WITH THE CONSEQUENCES OF OUR CHOICES AND ACTIONS.

things. It looks beyond today's clouds and awaits tomorrow's sunshine. I certainly learned patience while enduring the test of my faith. I didn't get into the situations that I was dealing with overnight; therefore, it would take more than a night for me to come through.

In my time of prayer, I prayed for wisdom. I needed the wisdom of God. I needed to know what God was doing through my trials.

In my darkest hour, I still remember the day my mother consoled me and spoke Proverbs 3:5-6 into my life. It seemed as if God himself spoke to me that day. I'll always remember those words, "Trust in the Lord with all your heart, And lean not on your own understanding; In all your ways acknowledge Him, And He shall direct your paths." A mother's love comforts, just as God's love comforts. It was her love that gave me hope. I began to accept the consequences of my actions and began to seek God for direction and understanding. I began to trust Him and His plan, even though some things were still unclear to me. I realize that just because we make some mistakes doesn't mean that God doesn't love us. We still have to deal with the consequences of our choices and actions.

There is a prize that awaits us after our trials. "Blessed is the man who endures temptation; for when he has been approved, he will receive the crown of life which the Lord has promised to those who love Him (James 1:12)." Never in a million years would I have fathom the blessings God would use to restore me. Remember, there is also hope for the future. God is a God of another chance. Even Jonah was given another chance to get it right.

CHAPTER 4

LIFE AGAIN

The storms of life come to interrupt our peace of mind. Often times it brings with it strong disturbances and attacks, sending our lives into a whirlwind. The blessing in the storm is that it comes to strengthen our walk with God and tests our faith. The Bible says that the suffering of this present time is not worthy to be compared to the glory that shall be revealed in us (Romans 8:18). The storm that Jonah experienced made him stronger and prepared him for the mission that God wanted him to fulfill.

"Now the word of the Lord came to Jonah the second time, saying, 'Arise, go to Nineveh, that great city, and preach to it the message that I tell you (Jonah 3:1-2).'" Just like Jonah, God came to me again and gave me another chance at life, love, and leadership. God did his greatest work when it was real dark in my life. When God was all that I had, I realized God was all that I needed.

> LIFE IS LIKE AN INTERSTATE. WHILE SOME PEOPLE EXIT OUR LIVES, THERE WILL BE SOME PEOPLE WHO WILL ENTER OUR LIVES.

After going through the divorce and experiencing the death of my mom and loss of my job, I went through yet another transition in my life. In order to progress through the transition, I needed a friend, and I found a friend in Iris

Jackson. She was a very attractive and business-savvy cosmetologist. She was independent and was on top of her game. She knew what she wanted in life and had a plan to achieve her goals. At the time, I needed someone to help me put things in order in my life. 1 John 4:8 says that God is love. Since this is true, wherever we find God, we will find love, and wherever we find love, we will find God. God's love truly saved my life. In the midst of things falling apart, I found love in Iris. Her love helped me refocus on God.

I knew Iris had to be heaven sent because she was the one who truly helped me with the transition of my mother going home to be with the Lord. She had

> SOME PEOPLE ARE ONLY IN OUR LIVES FOR A SEASON, BUT THEN, THERE ARE OTHERS WHO WILL BE A PART OF OUR LIVES FOR A LIFETIME.

the opportunity to meet my mom and had been around my family for a few months. When it's time for God to give us another chance, I think it is paramount that we be open and honest with God, ourselves and others. At that point, we have to accept responsibility for what we have done or what we have left undone. That is what I did when I first met Iris. I started our relationship by being honest with her about my past mistakes and the issues that I was dealing with during that time. I told her about my divorce, my daughters and the mistakes that I had made. I believe a shift took place in my life when I began to accept responsibility for the things that I had done and had left undone.

I had not been living the life that I had wanted to live or even planned to live, but God reminded me that I was not beyond hope. For many of us who have lived for a little while, we know that life doesn't always go according to how we plan. The good news is that God is looking for a group of imperfect people to use for His glory, to bless, and to show His almighty power.

When we are going through situations and are trying to move from one place to another, God will send people in our lives to help us. Life is like an interstate. While some people exit our lives, there

> IF A PERSON IS NOT A SAIL ON YOUR BOAT, THEN THEY MIGHT BE AN ANCHOR, HOLDING YOU DOWN.

will be some people who will enter our lives. Some people are only in our lives for a season, but then, there are others who will be a part of our lives for a lifetime. If a person is not a sail on your boat, then they might be an anchor, holding you down. Iris was definitely a sail, embracing life's winds and propelling us into our destiny in God.

It is important to have someone in our lives who sees the potential in the spirituality of where God wants to take us. Iris saw things in me that I did not see in myself at times. I really appreciate the encouragement that she gave me. Together we have been able to achieve great things. We are successfully parenting four beautiful and brilliant children, we have grown spiritually, and we have achieved financial goals. She is always there, pushing me and encouraging me. In relationships, we have to make critical decisions and it helps when we have someone there to help us.

Our success in life is dependent upon hearing God's voice. There were times that God would speak through Iris. That's why I share with other men that there are times that God will speak through our wives when we really don't know what to do. The converse is also true with wives and their husbands. God will sometimes allow a husband to confirm things for his wife when she needs direction. The Bible says that we have to be equally yoked. We have to be hearing the same thing and trying to accomplish the same goals. Iris has truly been my destiny and has helped realize my purpose in life.

In the thirteenth chapter of 1 Corinthians, the Bible tells us that love is patient and kind. It does not envy nor boast and is not proud. Love does not dishonor others and is not self-seeking. It always protects, always trusts, always hopes, and always perseveres. Love is powerful and life changing. My life has been blessed because of the love that I have received from not only Iris but also from my family and friends, such as my pastor, Bishop Darryl Brister, and my spiritual brother, Pastor Herbert Andrew. These two men kept me lifted in prayer and encouraged me to stand strong in the midst of adversity; they never gave up on me. Love truly saved my life in more ways than one.

I married Iris, and soon after, our first son Eric was born. I found employment and was working a regular corporate American job, working every day. Beyond her beauty, my wife is a woman of faith. I still remember getting a phone call from her one day while I was at work, telling me to bring home some boxes. When I

> OUR SUCCESS IN LIFE IS DEPENDENT UPON HEARING GOD'S VOICE.

asked what the boxes were for, she told me that we were getting ready to move. At the time, we were not in the market to buy a house. We hadn't really discussed making that next step either. Nevertheless, I brought home the boxes as she had asked. In our conversation, she shared with me that it was time for us to move. We were living in a quaint two-bedroom townhouse in Metairie, Louisiana. We were growing and our family was growing; therefore, we needed a place that could facilitate our growth.

Before going house hunting, my wife wrote down the type of house that she wanted. She wanted a four-bedroom house with an open floor plan, lots of windows and a big back yard. Habakkuk 2:2-3 says,

[2]"Write the vision
And make *it* plain on tablets,
That he may run who reads it.
[3] For the vision *is* yet for an appointed time;
But at the end it will speak, and it will not lie.
Though it tarries, wait for it;
Because it will surely come,
It will not tarry."

After writing the vision, we began to work our plan.

While I was living in Metairie, I was traveling back and forth to Hammond, Louisiana, every Sunday to assist Pastor Johnson who was the pastor of Beacon Light of Hammond. At one point, there was talk of me becoming the pastor Beacon Light of Hammond. It is evident today that God never planned for me to be there permanently. This is why we have to know and understand that what God has for us is for us, no matter what others may say. God will anoint us to be where he appoints us.

I continued to go to Hammond every Sunday to serve, but on one Sunday after looking for a house, I went Beacon Light of New Orleans instead of going to Hammond. I went to Bishop Brister's office when I arrived to let him know that I would be in service so that it wouldn't be a surprise to him. He was use to me being in Hammond. When I told him that I would be in service because Iris and I had been looking for a house, he asked how the process was going. I proceeded to tell him that we had found a nice house that we could afford. He responded by saying the real test was how my wife felt about the house. Iris really wasn't comfortable with the house. He said, "Son, listen, a house is about a woman." Bishop Brister went on to say that I was concerned about the price and everything else when my only concern should be making my wife happy. He told me to grab hold to my faith, step it up and find another house. I went out into service and told Iris about my conversation with Bishop Brister. After I told her what Bishop had said, she knew it was God. A few weeks later, we found the right house in Slidell, Louisiana. It was exactly like the house that my wife had described in her written vison.

In the process of moving, our second son Jalen was born. Things were starting to look up for my family and me. We bought our dream home, and our family now included our two sons and two daughters. We were doing well, but all of that was interrupted in the course of one day. After experiencing a devastating storm in the spiritual, I soon experienced it in the natural. A bad storm was predicted to hit Louisiana, but no one fathomed the damage and destruction that it would cause.

My family and I decided to go to Dallas to stay for a few days until the storm blew over. I thought that we were only going to be gone a few days and only packed a few jeans and a few shirts. We left all of our clothes, other belongings, and even a car in the garage.

On August 29, 2005, Hurricane Katrina made landfall in southeast Louisiana as a category 3 hurricane. It caused severe destruction along the Gulf coast from central Florida to Texas, much of it due to the storm surge. The most significant number of deaths occurred in New Orleans, Louisiana, which flooded as the levee system catastrophically failed; in many cases hours after the storm had moved inland. At least 1,833 people died in the hurricane and subsequent floods, making it the deadliest U.S. hurricane since the 1928 Okeechobee hurricane. The total property damage was estimated at $108 billion. The residual effects of this storm can still be seen in the city of New Orleans today, nearly ten years later. Needless to say, Hurricane Katrina caused us to lose everything that we had.

Losing all of our possessions in a natural disaster was a surreal experience. Many people were displaced and disconnected from their loved ones, friends and jobs. Death tolls were high, and there was no closure for many families because the remains of their loved ones were never found or were badly decomposed by the time they were identified. For the first time in my life, I had to request assistance from agencies like Red Cross and FEMA. We even received food stamps during this disaster period.

Once again I found myself asking God why tragedy came into my life. As I was trying to figure things out, God was working his plan. I remember staying with my brother-in-law in Texas at his house with 19 people living under one roof. I remember walking around the yard and God speaking to me. The Lord told me that some of what I was about to experience would be harvest and some would be favor. The harvest, he said, would come because I had sewn a lot. I had been a servant, working in ministry. He had seen my heart which was a servant's heart. He also said that some would be favor. In other words, the favor of God is going to open some doors and make some ways.

When we are experiencing certain situations in life, we shouldn't fight the process that God allows us to go through. It is a season of being where we are suppose to be and doing what we are suppose to do. The blessings and favor of God are going to be there. I know this all too well. While in Texas,

> GOD CAN'T USE US PUBLICALLY UNTIL HE HAS TRAINED US PRIVATELY.

God had a developmental plan for me, a strategy to get me to where he needed me to be. He was developing me into who he desired me to be.

Let's take a look at Elijah. Elijah had to face dried-up brooks just like many of us. God was preparing him for his physical and spiritual transformation. He was also preparing him for a place called "There." In 1 Kings 17:3, instructs Elijah to go to a place called "There" because He wanted to develop him into a mighty man of God. In other words, God was telling him that he couldn't use him publicly until He was trained privately. Often times we are in a rush to get "there" but sometimes God has to hid us and work on us "There." In verses three and four, God tells Elijah to go to the brook where He would take care of him. God did the same for my family.

Being in Texas was a time of separation for me. Sometimes in life, God has to separate us from some people and some things because He has to develop us into who he has purposed us to be. "Now the Lord had said to Abram: 'Get out of your country, from your family and from your father's house, to a land that I will show you (Genesis 12:1)."He had to get away from his kindred. Abraham thought that he needed Lot because he didn't have any children and Lot didn't have a father. "Then Lot chose for himself all the plain of Jordan, and Lot journeyed east. And they separated from each other (Genesis 13:11)." Just as God had to separate Abraham and Lot, He also separated me from some people, some things, and some situations. Sometimes God has to do the separating when we fail to depart. After Katrina, God allowed me to grow up. I found myself by myself, and that is when God showed me who I was.

Sometimes, when God does the separating, it seems as if we are left with the short end of the stick. If we learn to trust God for the outcome, it will change our outlook. Being set apart allows us to focus on the future. We have to move forward if we are going to receive everything that God has for us, regardless of our perception of things.

In the seventeenth chapter of 1 Kings, we see the transformation that Elijah goes through. In verse one, he is Elijah the Tishbite, but in verse twenty-four, he is Elijah a man of God. Elijah was able to mature during the season of his dried-up brook. We, too, will experience dry seasons, but that is when we should pray for God to allow us to grow and learn from our experiences.

Connections are very important. I had met a guy through Bishop Brister some years ago, and we developed a friendship. A few days after Katrina, he called me and asked me where I was. I

> IF WE LEARN TO TRUST GOD FOR THE OUTCOME, IT WILL CHANGE OUR OUTLOOK.

informed him that I was in Garland, TX which happened to be only 15 minutes away from where he lived. He came to check on my family and me to make sure we were okay.

A few days later, he called and said that he knew a man named Brian who wanted to be a blessing to those who suffered lost in Hurricane Katrina. He took me to this Brian's house. There were about six of us sitting around a table. God spoke to me and said that you have not because you ask not. While there, the Brian went to around the table and asks everyone what they needed. Some needed this, and others needed that. When he got to me, I asked for an outrageous amount of money. I asked for ten thousand dollars. He just looked at me and moved on. He left the house to go to the bank and returned with some cash. Brian gave one lady twenty-five hundred dollars, another he gave two thousand dollars, and he gave me twenty-five hundred dollars and some gift cards. I was very appreciative, and I thanked God for what he had done through this stranger. Before I left, I took two hundred and fifty dollars and gave it back to him and told him to put it in the offering at church as my tithes. I knew he was a Christian. That's why I believe in the principle of tithing also because God has a way of opening doors and making ways for us.

While we were riding in the car back to Garland, Texas, to my brother-in-law's house, the Brian's wife Tracy called. She said that she wanted to speak to the guy who was wearing the yellow shirt, me. She said that she had never met me before but she told her husband that the anointing that was on my life was so bright that she couldn't even stand to look at me. Because of that, she wanted to meet my wife. A few days passed by, and my wife and I returned to Louisiana to access the damage of the storm to our home in Slidell. None of our belongings were salvageable. We had at least five feet of water in our house. We lost clothing, furnishings, and a vehicle.

On our way back to Texas, I asked my wife if she had ever contacted the lady named Tracy. She said no, and I told her that we needed contact her. Tracy told my wife that she wanted us to come by her house we arrived back in Texas. We actually spent the night at her house, even though her husband was out of town.

The next day, her husband came back in town and drove me around town to look at houses. I told him that I wasn't ready to buy a house, and he then took me to some really nice apartments in a gated community. We went back to his house, and he told his wife to take my wife to look at the apartments. If she liked it, then they would take care of everything. We liked the apartments, and just as he had said, they took care of everything. They paid the deposits, twelve months of rent and completely furnished the apartment with furniture, appliances and everything that is needed for a house to function. They even bought my wife, children and me clothing.

Remember, I only asked for ten thousand dollars. What they actually gave us was probably valued at around thirty thousand dollars. God is able to do exceeding abundantly above all that we ask or think, according to the power that works in us. God had made provisions for my family and me in Texas, and I really thought it was our blessed place.

I eventually found a job there working for a company called Darden Restaurants which is the parent company for restaurants like Olive Garden, LongHorn Steakhouse, and Red Lobster. I was hired by the company, but I was not content with the salary that was offered to me. My supervisor at the time was Kevin Ross. He told me that he was unable to approve the salary that I requested and allowed me to talk to his boss. About five minutes after meeting with his boss, Kevin called me and said that I was approved for the salary that I had requested. Life couldn't get any better for me. I was living in my blessed place and begin to live again.

I felt like God had given me another chance at life. No one there knew my past and all of the mistakes that I had made. I thought that God had wiped the slate clean. Although God puts our sins in the sea of forgetfulness, some people chose to hold on to our past, reminding us of our shortcomings.

We were doing well. We were living in a beautiful three bedroom apartment. My wife and I both had our own cars. I was working for a great company, making good money. Within nine months, I was promoted to the next level on my job. There were people there who were saying that I didn't deserve my promotion. The Bible tells us that God will cause our enemies to become our footstools. Not only will God cause our enemies to become our footstools, but He will also prepare a table before us in the presence of our enemies (Psalm 23:5). He will use our enemies to take us to the next level. This was not common for this company. It took others seven to twelve years to accomplish what I did in just nine months. The favor of God was on me.

One day I had to go to the office to see where I was to relocate. I was being relocated to a place called Wichita Falls, TX. I thought this was it. I had moved up in the company, and my salary would increase to six figures. We were able to purchase our second home in Hurst, Texas, while still owning the first home that we purchased in Slidell. This is exactly how I had envisioned my life. My life was finally lining up with my plans. On the same day that I got promoted, I received a phone call from my pastor, Bishop Brister. He said, "Son, I need you to pastor Beacon Light of Baton Rouge." I said to myself, "No not right now." My pastor prayed for me while we were on the phone. When I got home, my wife was excited about my promotion. She wanted to know where were moving and how much money I would be making. In the same conversation, I had to tell her that I got a phone call from Bishop Brister, wanting us to move back to Louisiana to pastor Beacon Light of Baton Rouge. She said, "I know you said 'No!'"

I was confused. I didn't know whether to accept my promotion or pastor the church. There were no guarantees in pastoring a church. I had never led a congregation before. I didn't know anything about being a pastor. I accepted the promotion and moved to Wichita Falls, Texas. About five months later while working, I met an older Hispanic man who I worked with who would always tell me, "Mr. Eric, you don't belong here." He didn't know why, but he was certain that I didn't belong there. It was like God was confirming that it was time for me to move although I really didn't want to go back home to Louisiana. I was like Moses who was commanded by God to return to Egypt. "Come now, therefore, and I will send you to Pharaoh that you may bring My people, the children of Israel, out of Egypt (Exodus 3:10)."

I drove to Louisiana to see what the assignment was that God was calling me to do. The first Sunday that we came to Beacon Light of Baton Rouge there were thirty-five people present.

My wife leaned over to me and asked me if I had lost my mind. We went back to Texas. One night she told me if the Lord told me to move back to Louisiana then that was what we would do. Sometimes we have to sacrifice so that God can do what he has to do in our lives.

We moved back to Louisiana and began to pastor the church. In my past, it was said that ministry was over for me. To some degree, I thought that was true. God opened a door for me and I began to live life again in ministry because of obedience.

CHAPTER 5

FOCUSING ON THE FUTURE

Whether your challenge is drug addiction, alcoholism, loss of a job or loved one, sexual or financial issues or something else, don't allow your past or present condition define your future. We are never hopeless or beyond hope. When we begin to live again, we have to focus on the future. In order to focus on the future, we must remain humble. 1 Peter 5:6 tells us to humble ourselves under the mighty hand of God, and in due time, He will exalt us.

In my relationship with God, I had to learn that God will sometimes have to separate me from some people, places and things. The reality is that everyone is not going where we are going, and we have to stop feeling responsible for everyone. We will always be met with challenges when we attempt to take them into places that God never designed them to be. Then, God has to do the separating, just as He did with Abraham and Lot. Don't fight the process because the separation allows us to rise above all that weighs us down (drug addiction, alcoholism, financial issues, sexual issues, etc.) and allows us to live again.

Always remember the battle is not over until God says it's over. We are all over-comers, conquers. This was my thought process in moving back to Louisiana. I had to take an assessment of my life and make some corrections. The road back home was a place where I could live again. All conversions don't happen in church; some happen in the pig's pen, when we are down and out and in a mess. We have to make some conscious judgments and decisions to change various aspects of our lives in order to get to the place where God wants us to be. In 2006 on my wife's birthday, we made a critical, life changing decision. We decided to move back to Louisiana.

My early adulthood experiences and separation in Dallas were both a part of the preparation for my future. God gave me an opportunity to refocus and continue my journey. Every day that I woke up, I was looking for God to do something in my life. God knew that I would pastor a people in the Greater Baton Rouge area who would find hope and wisdom in my testimony. Becoming the pastor of Beacon Light of Baton Rouge is analogous to the union between a husband and wife. I find joy in ministering the gospel of Christ. It has been nothing but God's love that has allowed the ministry to grow from only a few members to over 2,000 in just seven short years. It's the love in our church that draws people.

> DON'T ALLOW YOUR PAST OR PRESENT CONDITION DEFINE YOUR FUTURE.

Don't doubt God. God has a plan for our lives, and at an appointed time, we will see the fruit of our labor if we don't faint. Let's take a look at Zacharias and Elizabeth, two just people who had an authentic relationship with God, yet it seemed as if God had forgotten about them. Zacharias was priest whose name means "the Lord will remember." His righteousness was seen in his both his public and private life, but he and his wife still had no child. Many would assume that his righteous was his pass to get whatever he wanted from God without even asking. That was not the case with Zacharias and Elizabeth; they had been praying for a very long time, just as many of us have been praying for a very long time. God told Zacharias that He is going to do what other people thought would never happen for him and his wife. Despite Zacharias's own personal negative assessment, God sent him an angel, Gabriel, to give him a heavenly assurance. God has done and is doing the same thing in our lives. He sends angels to encourage us doing our moments of doubt.

Zacharias needed an angel because he needed a heavenly assurance that God's promise would come to pass. His human assessment said that he had missed his opportunity to father a child because both he and his wife were of old age. Onlookers probably had a negative outlook on his situation as well. No matter how long the waiting period may last, we cannot doubt God. God caused Zacharias to become mute because he could not talk the language of faith. Sometimes we have to become mute and watch God. As long as we keep our eyes on Him, we can never lose focus of His promises for our lives. The first

> AS WE BEGIN TO LIVE AGAIN, YOU AND I WILL HAVE TO CONQUER OUR GIANTS IN OUR PROMISED LAND.

chapter of Luke proves that what God promises may not come when we want it to, but it will show up. After the nine-month pregnancy period, Zacharias and his wife gave birth to a son. Reaching our destiny is like giving birth to our promise. In that very moment, we realize that the sacrifice of the preparation and pain (the birthing process does cause pain) doesn't compare to the glory of the promise.

God knows and recognizes our human feelings. He knows that we get tired, frustrated, and, at times, even confused. That's why God will send people in our lives to guide, support, and encourage us. He sent Aaron to Moses, Jonathan to Saul, John to Peter, and Barnabas to Paul. We know there's a great deal in seeing the countenance of another. We see Christ's understanding for close relationships in His own life when John leans on His chest. With such closeness, Christ could whisper as he lay on His chest. In times of doubt, listen to your Gabriel.

It's true that you can't drive forward looking in the review mirror. No matter if your goals are short term or long term, don't lose focus of your destination by worrying about the past or present. I still deal with challenges on a daily basis, but God has blessed me to become more emotionally stable, spiritually stable and more stable in my relationships now that I have experienced some things and have gotten older. We make some mistakes along the way, just like the children of Israel. God made them a promise that they would go into the Promised Land; however, even in the midst of the getting there, they still had to face and defeat giants. As we begin to live again, you and I will have to conquer our giants in our Promised Land. Just as God has made promises to those of Biblical times, He has made some promises to you and me. Therefore, we must focus on the future. We must see our life's journey as preparation for the future.

I'll end this book just the way that I began it, talking about Jonah. God gave Jonah another chance to get things right despite his initial disobedience. Jonah's voyage to Ninevah was not one of personal gain. His mission, by design, was to save a people who were destined for destruction. God was using him for His glory. Jonah went into the city and proclaimed that the city would see destruction if the people did not change their ways within forty days. "So the people of Nineveh believed God, proclaimed a fast, and put on sackcloth, from the greatest to the least of them (Jonah 3:5)."

Jonah's ministry was so powerful that it even caused the king to change his heart.

"[6] Then word came to the king of Nineveh; and he arose from his throne and laid aside his robe, covered *himself* with sackcloth and sat in ashes. [7] And he caused *it* to be proclaimed and published throughout Nineveh by the decree of the king and his nobles, saying,

Let neither man nor beast, herd nor flock, taste anything; do not let them eat, or drink water. [8] But let man and beast be covered with sackcloth, and cry mightily to God; yes, let every one turn from his evil way and from the violence that is in his hands (Jonah 3:6-8)."

God saw the people of Ninevah and was pleased to see that they turned from their evil ways. He relented from the disaster that He had said He would bring upon them and did not do it. We see in Jonah's story that his obedience blessed the lives of the people of Ninevah. People were saved from destruction. When I apply the principle of focusing on the future to my personal life, I see God using me to help build His kingdom, just as he did with Jonah. We may not be perfect, but we have been chosen. Despite the challenges and storms that you may face in your life's journey, don't abort your promise. Use those same obstacles to propel you into your destiny. Never give up. There's life again.

Is there a book inside of you? Ever wanted to self publish but didn't know how? Concerned about the financial part of self publishing? Relax. Take a deep breath. We can help!

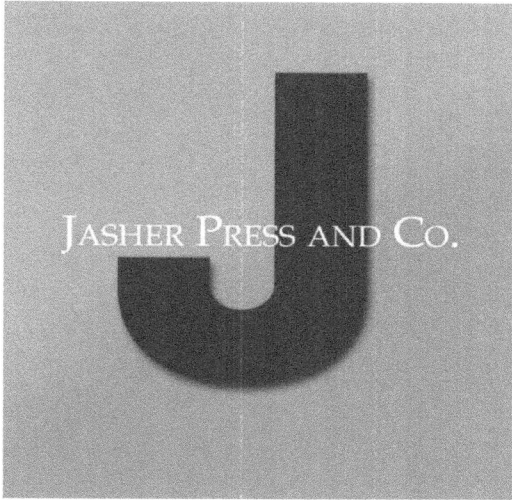

JASHER PRESS AND CO.

Finally! An affordable Self Publishing company for all of your Self Publishing needs. We have the right services, with the right prices with the right quality. So, what are you waiting for?

Unpack those dreams, break out that pen, your dreams of getting published may not be so far off after all!

Jasher Press & Co. is here to provide you with Consulting, Book Formatting, Cover Designs, editing services but most importantly inspiration to bring your dreams to past.

And this whole process can be done in less than 90 days! You thought about it, you talked about it but now is the time!

WWW.JASHERPRESS.COM
1-888-220-2068
CUSTOMERSERVICE@JASHERPRESS.COM

www.ingramcontent.com/pod-product-compliance
Lightning Source LLC
LaVergne TN
LVHW051815080426
835513LV00017B/1965